To Patrick & Krissie

[illegible signature]

10-2-95

Shreveport and Bossier City

FREDS
SOUTHERN
UNIVERSITY
METRO CENTER
LOUISIANA

SHREVEPORT AND BOSSIER CITY

PHOTOGRAPHS AND TEXT BY NEIL JOHNSON

WITH A FOREWORD BY JIM MONTGOMERY

LOUISIANA STATE UNIVERSITY PRESS
BATON ROUGE AND LONDON

This book is dedicated to the unselfish volunteers striving with limited energies and resources to push this community toward a greater good.

Manufactured in Korea
First Printing
04 03 02 01 00 99 98 97 96 95   5 4 3 2 1

Designer: Laura Roubique Gleason
Typeface: Janson Text
Printer and binder: Dai Nippon Printing Co., Ltd.

LIBRARY OF CONGRESS CATALOGING-IN-PUBLICATION DATA
Johnson, Neil, 1954–
Shreveport and Bossier City / photographs and text by Neil Johnson ; with a foreword by Jim Montgomery.
p. cm.
Includes index.
ISBN 0-8071-1995-4 (cloth : alk. paper)
1. Shreveport (La.) 2. Shreveport (La.)—Pictorial works. 3. Bossier City (La.) 4. Bossier City (La.)—Pictorial works.
I. Title.
F379.S4J64 1995
976.3'99—dc20   95-21115
CIP

The paper in this book meets the guidelines for permanence and durability of the Committee on Production Guidelines for Book Longevity of the Council on Library Resources. ∞

ACKNOWLEDGMENTS

Shreveport is my hometown. With Bossier City, it is a community of which I am proud to be a part. I am prouder still to have been given the opportunity by LSU Press to do a book about it.

A large majority of these photographs were made during the first half of the 1990s. As our deadline approached, the community began to go through a period of dramatic growth and change. The original publication date was even postponed a year so that the changes occurring during 1994 could be included.

This is a book of contemporary Shreveport and Bossier City. But because the present is a summation of the past, I turned to a respected historian for assistance in making sure the captions' many historical details were absolutely as accurate as possible. My heartfelt thanks go to Eric Brock, my able guide through that fascinating—though often deceptive—place called history.

Even though this book was produced in the middle of a technological revolution in which photography began merging with computers, not a single image in the book has been digitally altered in any way.

A place—any place—cannot be fully understood without looking down on it to gain a "big picture" perspective. A number of pilots carried me aloft so I could produce aerial images. My thanks to hot air balloon pilots Ken Wojcik and Pat and Susan Harwell, to Spanky McCoy for his helicopter rides, and to Jim Walker for his fixed-wing skills.

And, finally, there can never be satisfactory closure for a project like this. I reluctantly send it to press with strong feelings of pride mixed with some frustration that so many facets of this community were left out due to time, space, or logistical constraints. I turn it over now to the very talented team at LSU Press, who have been a joy to work with from day one.

NEIL JOHNSON

CONTENTS

CBD Central Business District

- Caddo Parish Courthouse
- Civic Theater
- Commercial Tower
- Harrah's Casino
- McNeill Street Pumping Station
- Municipal Auditorium
- Oakland Cemetery
- Riverfront Park
- Scottish Rite Cathedral
- Shreve Memorial Library
- SporTran Terminal
- Spring Street Museum
- Strand Theatre
- Texas Street Bridge
- United States Court House

Shreveport/Bossier City Outside Central Business District

1. American Rose Center
2. AT&T's Shreveport Works
3. Atlas Processing Company
4. Barksdale Air Force Base
5. Boothill Speedway
6. Bossier City Municipal Complex
7. Bossier Parish Community College
8. Centenary College & Meadows Museum
9. Champion Lake
10. Fair Grounds Field
    Independence Stadium
    Louisiana State Exhibit Museum
    Louisiana State Fairgrounds
11. General Motors Assembly Plant
12. Hamel's Amusement Park
13. Horseshoe Casino
14. Isle of Capri Casino
15. Kansas City Southern Rail Yard
16. Libbey Glass
17. Louisiana Downs
18. LSU in Shreveport
19. LSU Medical Center
    Biomedical Research Center
    Shriners Hospital for Crippled Children
20. Norton Art Gallery
21. Overton Brooks VA Medical Center
22. Pioneer Heritage Center
23. Port of Shreveport-Bossier
24. Schumpert Medical Center
25. Southern University at Shreveport
26. Walter B. Jacobs Nature Park
27. Willis-Knighton Medical Center

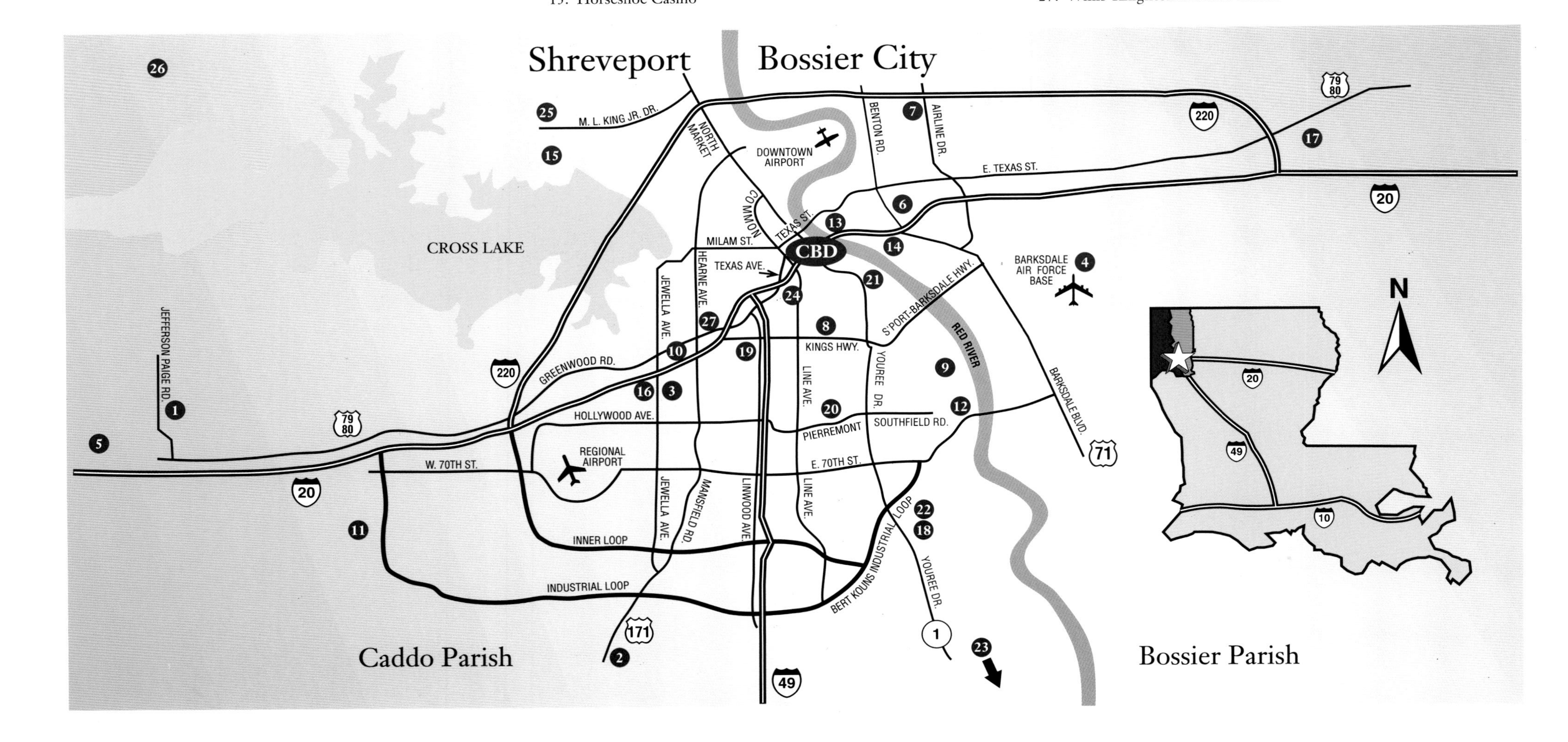

FOREWORD

A traveler coming through the two largest cities of northwest Louisiana could well find himself on East Texas Street in Bossier City, crossing the Red River onto Texas Street in Shreveport, and wonder which state this is, really. Welcome to "the other Louisiana," where "the Deep South meets the West." That phrase was a local slogan years ago, one of many conjured by civic boosters through the decades to try to describe exactly what characterizes us. No single phrase seems to do the job. Our symbols range from roses to racetracks and riverboat casinos. Although our traditions are as cherished as an antique gaslight, we don't hesitate to add a little modern neon and glitter to them. This book catches the look and feel of it all at a particular moment, even as time and changes pass the moment by and make it a part of our history.

The settlement that grew up to become Shreveport was born in the 1830s as the result of a massive United States government project to open the Red River for navigation, and in its infancy was a private business founded by outside investors. As we enter the twenty-first century, the Shreveport–Bossier City region is headed for new economic life as the result of a massive United States Army Corps of Engineers project to re-open the Red for navigation, and outside investors are mainstays of our future. You might say, "The more things change, the more they stay the same," but during the intervening years, a lot has happened to make this part of the Pelican State decidedly—some might say "cussedly"—different from the better-known Cajun and New Orleans regions of South Louisiana.

One reason for the differences, and a reason some visitors claim we seem "more like East Texas," has to do with when we were settled and by whom. South Louisiana's culture is French-Spanish and Roman Catholic in origin, and the first French settlers arriving in the early 1700s—before the United States existed as a nation—came only as far north as Natchitoches. It was more than a century later that the first non-native settlers came to the rest of northwest Louisiana, and they were already Americans when they got here—after the Louisiana Purchase in 1803 and Louisiana statehood in 1812—as part of the early westward migration in the burgeoning young nation. Many of them came from the Piedmont and Appalachian regions and were of Scotch-Irish Protestant descent. Some stopped here, while their relatives kept going a few miles west to settle in Texas—so not only are the North Louisiana/East Texas red-clay-and-pine-trees physical settings similar, we're culturally the same. The last century and a half has brought thousands of people of other nationalities and races to our cities, adding different ethnic, religious, and social ingredients to the mix, but those early settlers set the patterns that make us a place where you're more likely to find Texas barbecue than Louisiana boudin—although the boudin's here, if you look for it.

Before all of that, there were the Native Americans—in our case, the Caddo Indians, for whom Caddo Parish is named. They owned all the land in the early nineteenth century, when the federal government wanted to encourage western expansion along the region's rivers. The Caddos were friendly, but the Red River wasn't. It was jammed for about 160 miles by the Great Raft, a snarl of driftwood, silt, logs, and whole trees that the treacherous river had chewed loose from its banks. The government hired Captain Henry Miller Shreve for the seemingly impossible task of clearing it. He started in 1833, using steam-powered "snagboats" of his own invention, opened a navigable channel within two years, and finished the job before the decade was over. During that time, for $80,000, the Caddos sold all their land to the United States government, with the stipulation that an early trader named Larkin Edwards could choose any 640 acres of it for his own. It was on the Edwards tract that a group of real estate speculators—including Captain Shreve—formed the Shreve

Town Company as a private business. In 1837 they renamed the place Shreveport, and two years later it was incorporated and chartered as a town by the state of Louisiana. The original street grid laid out by the Shreve Town Company is what we now know as downtown Shreveport. Those streets, incidentally, also reveal the Texas influence. Downtown's main thoroughfare, revamped and redecorated in the 1990s, is named Texas Street—because it was the start of the trail settlers used when they got off the early riverboats and headed west. You'll also find Milam, Fannin, Travis, and Crockett—as in Davy—all named for heroes of the Texas Revolution.

The colorful history of those early days is recorded in more detail in other texts. For our purposes, suffice it to say that we began as a frontier river town, for a time the westernmost city in the United States, and things were barroom-tough. The first preacher who tried to hold a church service here was roughed up by the rowdies, but it didn't take long for civilization to set in, so that today Shreveport sometimes calls itself "a city of churches."

During the Civil war, the young town sent soldiers to fight elsewhere, but the war didn't scar Shreveport as much as it did the rest of the South, with battles reaching only to the southern outskirts of the area. As Union troops took over much of the rest of the state, however, the Confederate Louisiana capital was moved from the south to safer ground at the Caddo Parish Courthouse. The last surrender of Confederate Louisiana's armaments—some say the last arms of the Confederacy—took place on the courthouse square.

During Reconstruction, there were attempts for this area to secede from Louisiana and be annexed into Texas. Northwest Louisianians, never particularly fond of Louisiana state government, were particularly vehement in their dislike of the Reconstruction version, and the feeling was apparently mutual. A Shreveport *Times* editorial of the period noted that Governor William Pitt Kellogg "considers us a hard case." Shreveport leaders also wished to join forces with their culturally similar East Texas neighbors, some of whom were willing to annex Caddo and other nearby parishes. That effort might have succeeded except for a gruesome interruption. A yellow fever epidemic in 1873 killed 760 of the young city's 4,000 people, and some formerly friendly Texans set up barricades to keep out any infected Shreveport travelers. The city worried more about staying alive than about its governmental jurisdiction, and by the time it had recovered, Reconstruction was ending, so we stayed in Louisiana.

Meanwhile, across the river was Bossier Parish, which was named for Pierre Evariste Bossier, a congressman when the parish was formed in 1843. At the southern end of the parish, directly opposite Shreveport, was a rural settlement called Cane's Landing. It was incorporated in 1907 as Bossier City. The name originally had a French pronunciation, but it's now "Boze-yer," and it's one of the fastest-growing cities in the state.

While there is municipal competition between them, together the two cities have grown to be one of the state's largest urban centers, the largest in North Louisiana, and the unofficial capital of a region known as the Ark-La-Tex, where the corners of Arkansas, Louisiana, and Texas meet.

River transportation made their early growth possible, but by the late nineteenth century railroads were eclipsing the steamboats. In the twentieth century the trains in turn lost large chunks of their trade to the highways—especially after Interstate 20 came through east to west, once again connecting us more closely to Texas than to the rest of Louisiana. Only with completion of Interstate 49 in 1996 will Shreveport and Bossier City finally have their first interstate-highway connection to South Louisiana. Air travel came to the region in the 1920s, when then-new Delta Airlines made Shreveport one of its first destinations, and has grown in both passenger and freight service through the years. Today the circle is complete, with all four modes of transportation arrayed to contribute to our continuing success: the Red River Navigation project, completed in 1995, with a new Caddo-Bossier Port and industrial park; regional rail facilities; Shreveport Regional Airport and Downtown Airport; and the completion of major highways crossing here. It's natural that the area is becoming a regional distribution center, and we're now an international port of entry for the U.S. Customs Service.

Agriculture was important at the beginning and still is, with timber, cotton, and soybean farming, but the area's real wealth came with the discovery of huge oil and natural gas fields in the early twentieth century. Later the economy diversified into manufacturing, with General Motors, General Electric, Poulan/Weed Eater, and AT&T among our prominent employers. A new wave of industrial technology could well be developed here through just-beginning research in robotics and micromanufacturing.

As we enter a new century, our spotlighted growth industry is medicine and health care. Schumpert and Willis-Knighton Medical Centers, the Louisiana State University Medical Center, Bossier General Hospital, and Doctors Hospital have made us a regional medical center, and we also have specialized facilities such as our first-in-the-nation Shriners Hospital for Crippled Children and the Veterans Administration Medical Center. Our newest entity, developed as an economic initiative by civic leaders—who raised private donations, got a local tax passed, won federal grants, and achieved state cooperation—is the nonprofit Biomedical Research Institute of Northwest Louisiana, which sits side by side with Louisiana State University Medical School in Shreveport.

Higher education here includes not just the Medical School but also Louisiana State University in Shreveport, Southern University at Shreveport, Bossier Parish Community College, and satellite programs of Louisiana Tech University, all in the public sector, and Centenary College as a renowned private liberal-arts institution supported by the United Methodist Church.

A significant employer, as well as a source of regional pride, is Barksdale Air Force Base on the Bossier City side of the river. Another big Bossier business and attraction is Louisiana Downs, which offers thoroughbred racing—including the Grade I Stakes Super Derby—for much of the year. Newer, but already drawing hundreds of thousands of visitors, are the three riverboat casinos that now offer twenty-four-hour dockside gaming on both riverbanks—Harrah's on the Shreveport side and Horseshoe and Isle of Capri in Bossier City. They form the core of the area's growing tourism industry, which both cities are working to develop still more, particularly in the realms of professional entertainment and sports.

Part of the tourism effort will no doubt rely on some more history. Back in the early 1900s, Shreveport was home to a legal red-light district, reputedly the largest for a city its size in the nation. While we might not want to bring that back, we do want to pay homage to some of the musicians who played in that district—notably Huddie "Leadbelly" Ledbetter, the "King of the 12-String Guitar." And not for nothing did Jelly Roll Morton compose a ragtime tune titled "Shreveport Stomp."

Even better known is the heritage of the "Louisiana Hayride." Broadcast weekly from Shreveport's Municipal Auditorium, the show in its 1940s and 1950s heyday gave career starts to such performers as Hank Williams Sr., Johnny Horton, and a young truck driver named Elvis Presley.

Just to show it wasn't all blues and country, Shreveport is also the birthplace and childhood home of pianist Van Cliburn, who began his concert career with the Shreveport Symphony, which is now Louisiana's oldest continuously performing professional orchestra. We also have one of the nation's oldest continuing community theaters, the Shreveport Little Theatre. Then there are the award-winning Marjorie Lyons Playhouse at Centenary College, the Shreveport Opera, several dance companies, the East Bank Community Theater, and the Bossier Parish Community College Cavalier Players. The rejuvenated Shreveport riverfront is home to the Shreveport Civic Theater and several convention facilities, and the Bossier Civic Center hosts a variety of events. The crown jewel of the performing arts is the beautiful neobaroque Strand Theatre in downtown Shreveport, now a hall for touring shows and professional entertainers after a nonprofit organization acquired it and shepherded it through a multimillion-dollar restoration in the 1980s.

Museums showcase a variety of art, including the outstanding American Western paintings and sculpture at the Norton Art Gallery and the unique collection of paintings done in pre–World War II Southeast Asia by Jean Despujols, which is housed at the Meadows Museum. The Louisiana State Exhibit Museum offers visitors both art and cultural history.

The Sports Museum of Champions, on the other

hand, helps illustrate the area's love of athletics. In addition to collegiate and prep teams, we're home to professionals—whose names also show the mixed culture: the Texas League baseball Captains, the Continental Basketball Association Storm, and the Canadian—yes, Canadian—Football League Pirates. We're also host, each December, to postseason college football in the Independence Bowl.

Our Louisiana heritage does show up in at least one obvious way, in that we like our festivals. We're home to the annual Louisiana State Fair, the Red River Revel arts festival, the annual Holiday in Dixie spring festival, the Good Times festival celebrating African-American heritage, and yes, even one for the Louisiana crawfish—our annual Mudbug Madness festival. Our Mardi Gras celebration is young compared with its South Louisiana predecessors but grows in raucous splendor each year.

We conduct all this business and frivolity in a setting graced by numerous beautiful residential, commercial, public, and religious buildings. A state historic preservation officer once referred to downtown Shreveport as "a little Manhattan" because of its astonishing variety of architectural styles. We're home to hundreds of churches, including cathedrals for both the Episcopal and Roman Catholic faiths. Our neighborhoods, whether along Fairfield Avenue with its grand mansions or in districts with less spectacular homes, often cause visitors to remark, "It's so green!" We live in forests, even in the middle of town.

We're also, thanks to concerted efforts of local business and civic activists, the national headquarters of the American Rose Society, which is housed in the American Rose Center and its acres of gardens. When the roses aren't blooming, the center transforms its grounds into a spectacular light show from Thanksgiving to New Year's as part of "December on the Red," when both cities display holiday lighting finery from the riverfronts to the suburbs.

Two cities joined by one river also have another obvious category of features—bridges. There are spans connecting us at six points. One of them, popularly known as the Texas Street Bridge, has been adopted as our symbol of unity, since it's the link that ties Bossier City's East Texas Street to Shreveport's Texas Street. The bridge is old and historic, but the Shreveport Regional Arts Council persuaded government and business to work together not long ago to update it and make it shine, literally: we put a red, pink, and orange neon light sculpture on it, added searchlights on both ends, strung fiber optic cables across it on the Shreveport side, and fired green argon lasers off it right down the middle of Texas Street—the same trail blazed by the old settlers. They might not recognize it now, but they'd surely be proud.

Neil Johnson's outstanding work in capturing all of this—the people, places, and flavors, the flowers, the lights, and the neighborhoods—is the work of someone who loves his native community. He has taken pictures of them over and over, watching them grow and recording the changes. He's also helped bring about some of those changes through his own involvement in civic committees and task forces. His photographs are prominently displayed at the airport to welcome visitors and are seen in numerous private collections. He has also been published in several volumes that received national distribution. Johnson's photography captures the wide scope of modern Shreveport and Bossier City, but it also homes in on the faces and personalities that bring the true flavors of life to our region. A primeval lake at sunset catches his attention, and so do the celebrating smiles of children at a festival or the excited shouts of gamblers in a casino. Knowing he was attempting to picture Shreveport and Bossier City at a time of rapid transition, Johnson pushed deadlines to the limit, getting "just one more shot" of a redeveloped downtown or a new class at the LSU School of Medicine. His efforts have created a comprehensive, up-to-date view of our cities—and one that's also beautiful.

Neil Johnson knows, and has caught with lens and light, "the other Louisiana" at this moment in its history.

JIM MONTGOMERY

SHREVEPORT AND BOSSIER CITY

COMMERCIAL TOWER, AMERICAN TOWER

The large flag atop the Premier Bank Building is reflected in the American Tower, with the Commercial Tower in the background.

(Overleaf) RED RIVER, DOWNTOWN SHREVEPORT

The banks of the Red River near downtown Shreveport underwent drastic changes in 1994 with the completion of Shreveport's new Riverfront Park and the arrival of three riverboat casinos, one in Shreveport and two in Bossier City, including the Isle of Capri Casino in the foreground of this view.

WRAY-DICKINSON BUILDING

A terra-cotta lion and winged wheels top the facade of the Wray-Dickinson Building on Market Street. Designed by Edward Neild, the building was erected in 1915 to house the Wray-Dickinson Ford dealership.

Ground fog blankets southeast Shreveport.

(Right) Isle of Capri Casino

STREETSCAPE

Shreveport's Central Business District underwent a dramatic transformation in the early 1990s. Streets were replaced, sidewalks widened, lighting improved, and benches, trees, and public art installed to make the area much more comfortable for pedestrians. The district's centerpiece is the unusually wide Texas Street.

SPRING STREET MUSEUM

Antiques and artifacts from the community's past are on display in the Spring Street Museum, one of Shreveport's oldest surviving buildings. Built as a bank in 1865, it is the only local building with its original cast-iron balcony still intact.

(Left) BLUE HERON, CROSS LAKE

On the northwestern side of Cross Lake, a great blue heron enjoys breakfast.

(Overleaf) LAKE BISTINEAU

Lake Bistineau, southeast of Bossier City, provides a quintessentially Louisianian setting in which to cool off on water skis, reel in a few bass, or just enjoy a summer evening slowly cruising the cypress-lined channels by houseboat.

COTTON INDUSTRY

Cotton is no longer "king" in the South, but it is still a key crop in the rich bottomlands of the Red River, some of the most fertile farmland in America. The field being harvested here lies just outside Shreveport's southern city limits.

4

(Above and right) CENTENARY COLLEGE

The serene campus of Centenary College of Louisiana gives little hint of the school's nomadic past. Founded in 1839 in Clinton, Mississippi, Centenary moved to Jackson, Louisiana, in 1845, taking over the facilities of the College of Louisiana (founded 1825), which had closed that year. In 1908, after the major rail routes bypassed Jackson, the college relocated to Shreveport.

Affiliated with the United Methodist Church, Centenary provides not only higher education to students from throughout the region, but also cultural enrichment to the community by way of the Meadows Museum of Art, the Hurley School of Music, the Centenary College Choir, and the Marjorie Lyons Playhouse.

MEADOWS MUSEUM

The Meadows Museum of Art at Centenary College is the permanent home of the internationally acclaimed Jean Despujols collection of paintings and drawings of Indochina. These works, created during the 1930s, offer a rare portrayal of the pre–World War II civilizations of Vietnam, Laos, and Cambodia. Despujols, a French artist, made Shreveport his home from 1941 until his death in 1965. The Meadows Museum also has an active exhibition schedule of other works of art.

ANTIOCH BAPTIST CHURCH

Located on Texas Avenue, which was once part of the old Texas Trail, a major overland route to the West, the Antioch Baptist Church is the oldest African-American Baptist church in Shreveport. Organized in 1866, the congregation moved to this building in 1903. The Romanesque Revival structure was designed by local architect N. S. Allen.

In the first half of the 1900s, this section of Texas Avenue was a center of local black business, cultural, and social activity. Louis Armstrong, Count Basie, and Duke Ellington were among the performers who appeared in the clubs and dance halls along "the Avenue."

BOSSIER CITY HOME WITH PECAN TREES

Large sections of south Bossier City were once pecan orchards. Today many of the old trees shade suburban houses.

I-20/LA. 1 INTERCHANGE

The area's main east-west artery, Interstate 20, connects with Louisiana Highway 1, for many years the main route to South Louisiana.

(Overleaf) PORT OF SHREVEPORT-BOSSIER

A distribution center for the import/export of oil and gas, grain, raw goods, and manufactured products by way of the Red River, the Port of Shreveport-Bossier brings back into the local economic mix the inexpensive water transportation that led to Shreveport's founding in 1835. Located just south of Shreveport, the port is governed by the Caddo-Bossier Port Commission.

LOCK AND DAM NO. 5

These structures are the nearest to Shreveport of the numerous engineering works that, by 1995, had tamed the Red River, opening the once-unpredictable stream to regular navigation.

KWANZAA

The bright colors of traditional African attire enliven Kwanzaa, a nationwide seven-day celebration of the unique heritage of African Americans. Kwanzaa, meaning "first fruits," is held from December 26 through January 1, with each day devoted to a specific principle, such as unity, creativity, or faith.

SYMPHONY HOUSE

Built in 1872 at the intersection of McNeill and Fannin Streets, this house was moved by the Shreveport Symphony Guild to its present location on Woodlawn across from Centenary College in 1956. Now known as the Symphony House, it was the first local building to be listed on the National Register of Historic Places.

POULAN/WEED EATER

An engineer at Poulan/Weed Eater uses a computer to assist in designing a power tool. The company, the world's leading manufacturer of hand-held electric, gasoline, and battery-powered lawn and garden equipment, has its headquarters in Shreveport, along with its divisions of distribution, engineering, and sales.

SCHUMPERT MEDICAL CENTER

Schumpert Medical Center originated as an infirmary of Shreveport surgeon T. E. Schumpert in 1894. In 1908 Schumpert Sanitorium was given to the Sisters of Charity of the Incarnate Word, who moved it to the present location just off Fairfield in 1911 and continue to own and operate the facility. A Cancer Treatment Center was dedicated in 1990.

MARDI GRAS

While Mardi Gras is part of the culture in South Louisiana, it has led an on-again, off-again existence in Shreveport and Bossier City. These days it's on-again, with a full Carnival season complete with masked balls and showers of beads and doubloons. The largest event, the Gemini Parade, winds its way from one side of the river to the other the Saturday before Fat Tuesday.

ARTBREAK

ArtBreak, the largest children's festival in the state, features visual-arts exhibits and performing arts from students throughout Caddo Parish. Founded in 1984, it is sponsored by the Shreveport Regional Arts Council, a division of Shreveport Parks and Recreation.

(Overleaf and above) NORTON ART GALLERY

The R. W. Norton Art Gallery, opened in 1966 on Creswell Street near the Uptown Shopping Center, shelters American and European paintings, sculpture, and decorative arts spanning more than four centuries. Its most renowned collections are those of works by Western artists Frederic Remington and Charles M. Russell. The sculpture in the foreground here is Remington's *Coming Through the Rye.*

Each spring the art has a serious rival for visitors' attention when 11,000 azalea plants explode into bloom on forty acres of landscaped gardens surrounding the gallery. The gardens are open to the public year round.

LOUISIANA DOWNS

Opened in 1974 in Bossier City, Louisiana Downs thoroughbred racetrack offers main-track racing as well as a turf course. The track is home to the state's only Grade I race, the nationally respected Super Derby. Racing season is from spring into early fall.

Louisiana Downs

I-20/I-49 interchange under construction

PIONEER HERITAGE CENTER

The Pioneer Heritage Center, a living-history museum on the LSU–Shreveport campus, features six carefully restored buildings brought from area plantations and settlements over several years, beginning in 1977. Two of the structures, the Caspiana House and the log dogtrot cabin, both shown here, were built before the Civil War.

RED RIVER RADIO

Public radio in northern Louisiana, southern Arkansas, and eastern Texas originates at KDAQ, located on the LSU–Shreveport campus. By relaying its signal to KLSA in Alexandria, KBSA in El Dorado (Arkansas), and KLDN in Lufkin (Texas), the station can reach a potential audience of 2 million. KDAQ offers National Public Radio news and classical, jazz, and blues music and is the only totally listener-supported station in the region.

BARRET PLACE

The Barret Place mansion on Fairfield Avenue was built in 1908 by future lieutenant governor Thomas C. Barret. It either replaced or expanded the house built in 1866 by W. W. Barret. The property has remained in the same family to this day.

CONFEDERATE MONUMENT

Erected in 1905 by the United Daughters of the Confederacy, the granite monument, between the Caddo Parish Courthouse and Texas Street, is a memorial to the Confederate soldiers who died during the Civil War.

UNITED
DAUGHTERS
OF THE
1905

LSU MEDICAL CENTER AND SHRINERS HOSPITAL

The LSU Medical Center *(background)* consists of the LSU Hospital, LSU School of Medicine and the School of Allied Health, and the School of Graduate Studies. The facility also specializes in the treatment of life-threatening trauma and has the only burn center in the area.

The Shriners Hospital for Crippled Children *(foreground)*, the first Shriners hospital in the country, opened its doors in 1922 on this same site. The new building replaced the original in 1986.

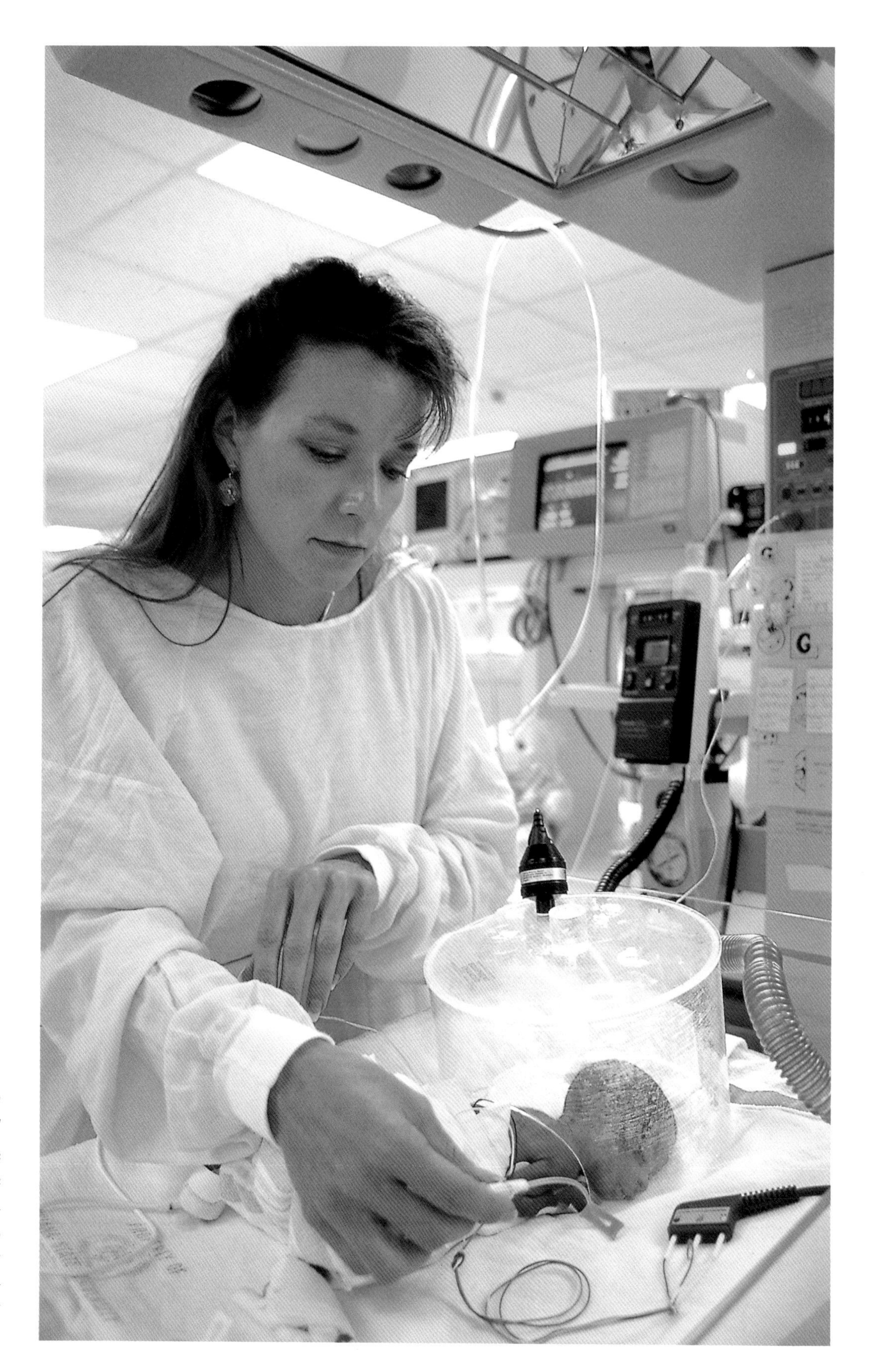

NEONATAL ICU,
LSU HOSPITAL

The Neonatal Intensive Care Unit in the LSU Hospital, the university teaching hospital for the LSU Medical Center, treats the many serious medical problems associated with the area's high rate of premature births.

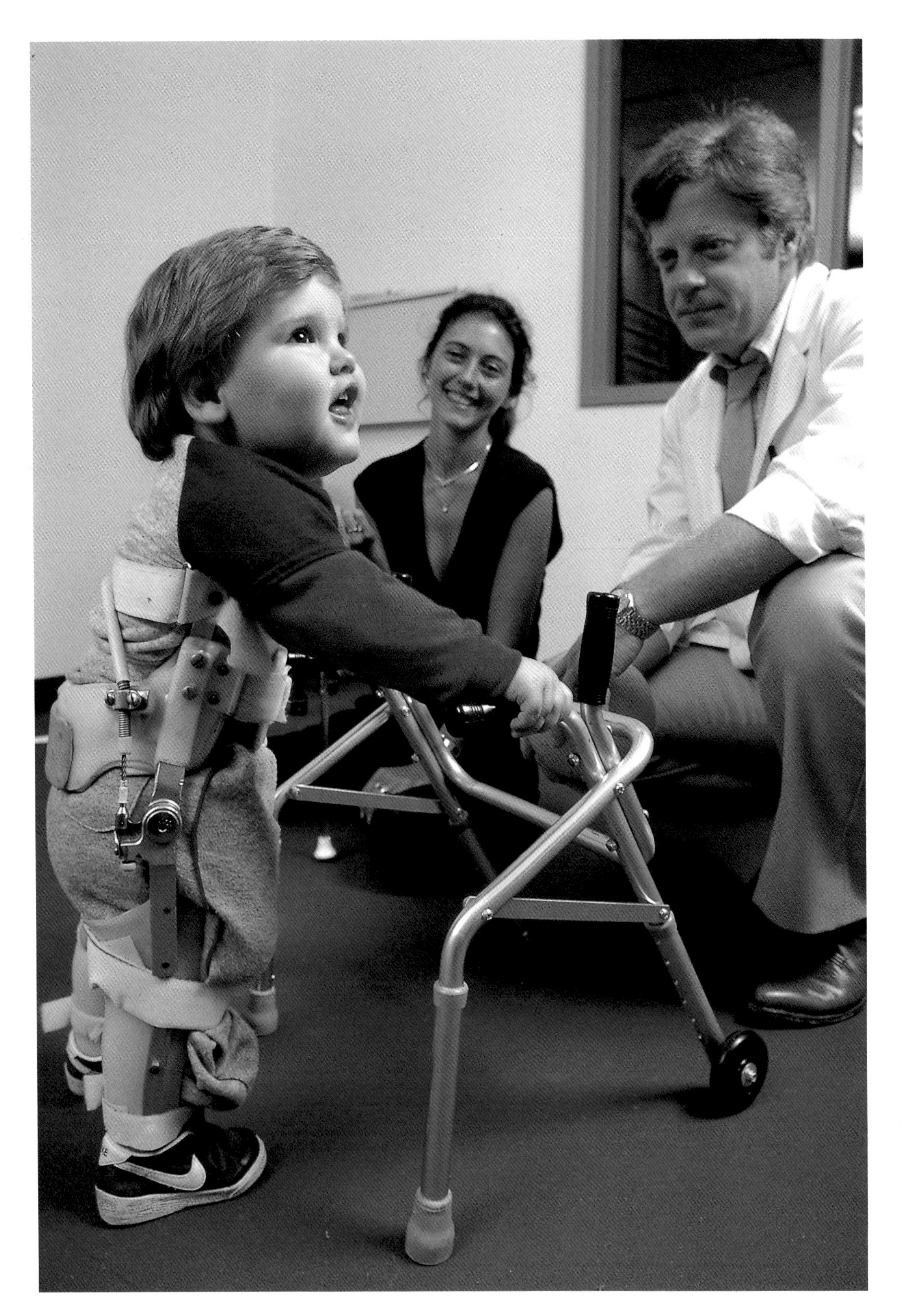

ORTHOPEDIC CARE, SHRINERS HOSPITAL

Much of the mission of the Shriners Hospital involves orthopedic medical care. Through charitable donations and the service work of the Shriners, the hospital gives its services free of charge.

BIOMEDICAL RESEARCH INSTITUTE

Pioneering Shreveport's newest industry, biotechnology, the Biomedical Research Foundation opened its first research facility, the Biomedical Research Institute, in 1994. In fifty-six state-of-the-art laboratories, institute scientists conduct research into new medical technology, techniques, and drugs. Located adjacent to the LSU Medical Center, the institute houses the first positron emission tomography (PET) imaging center in the region.

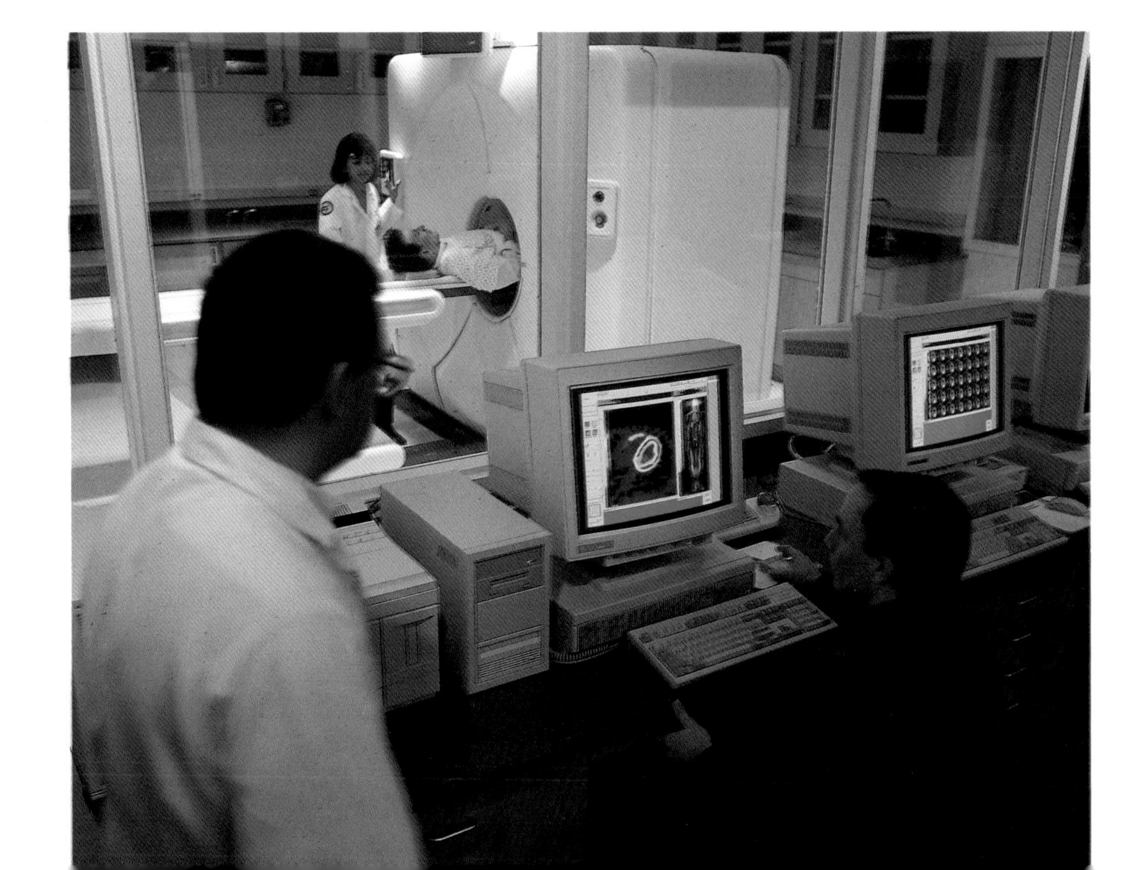

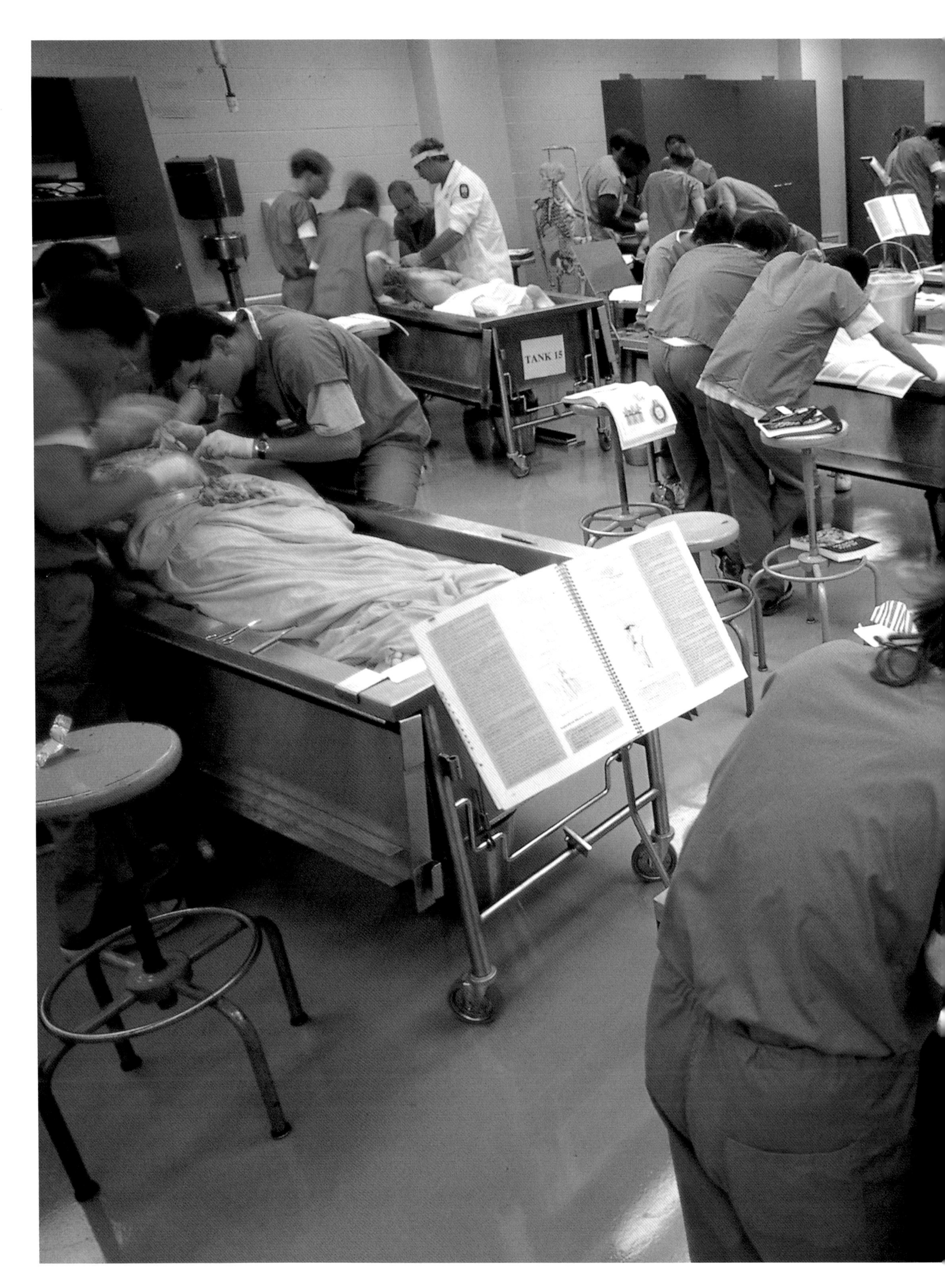
TANK 15

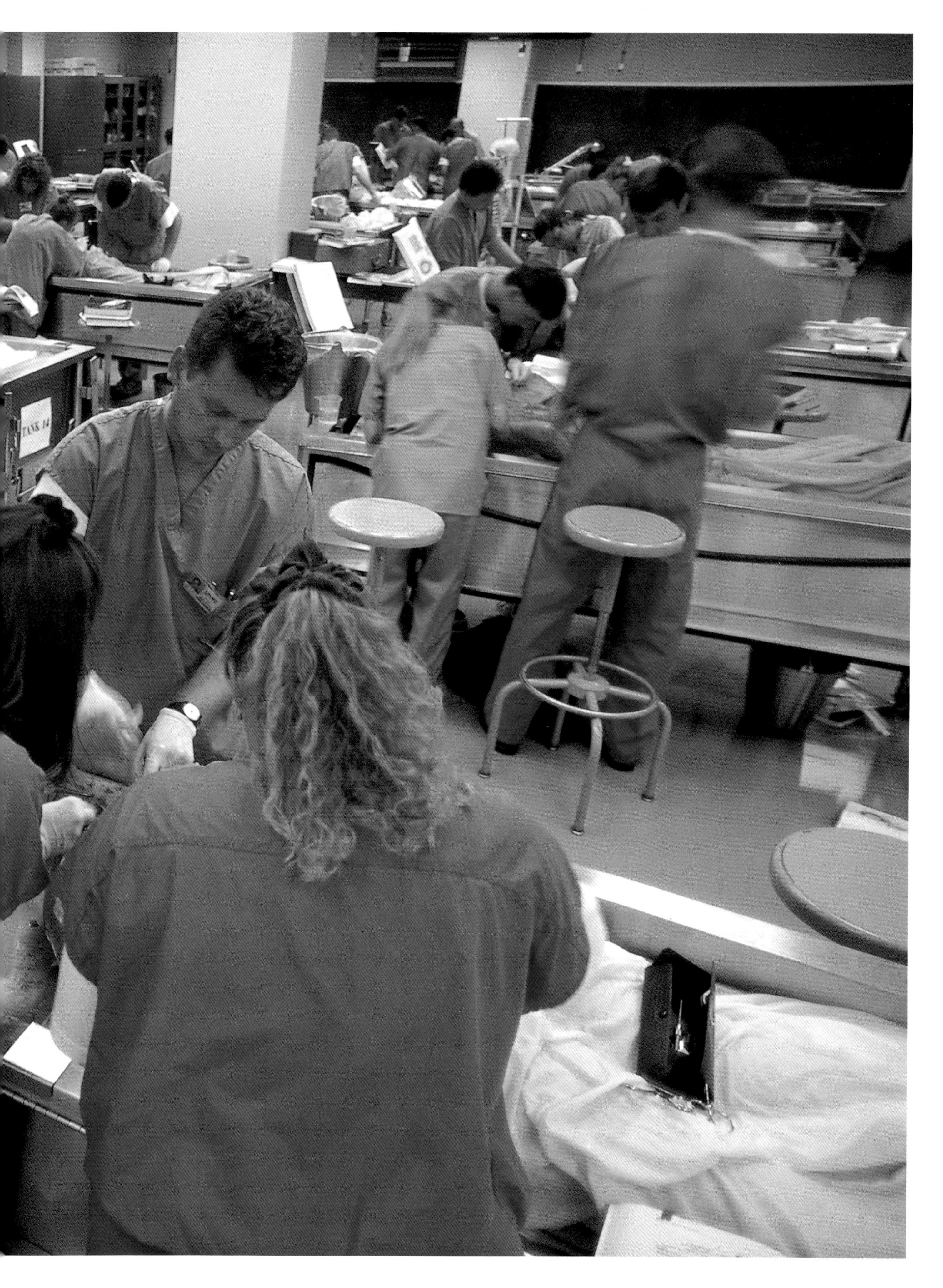
TANK 14

MARJORIE LYONS PLAYHOUSE

The Marjorie Lyons Playhouse is home to Centenary College's Department of Theater, Speech and Dance. Primarily a teaching theater for Centenary students, the program also uses many other local actors in its casts. Here, the scientist cowers before his creation in a staging of *Frankenstein*.

The community has long enjoyed a wealth of performing talent in both dramatic and musical theater, as evidenced by the number of theaters and acting troupes. The Shreveport Little Theatre, on Margaret Place, is among the oldest continuously producing community theaters in the country.

(Overleaf) LSU SCHOOL OF MEDICINE IN SHREVEPORT

On the first day of anatomy class, medical students begin their hands-on experience of working with the human body. As part of the LSU Medical Center, the LSU School of Medicine in Shreveport educates future physicians to help meet the health care needs of the area and state. The school also conducts medical research and provides a base for the continuing education of area physicians.

PETER PAN PLAYERS

The Peter Pan Players, founded in 1973, is a children's theater company for ages four through seventeen. The group performs several plays per year and conducts creative-dramatics classes each summer.

FIRST METHODIST CHURCH/AVN

A part of the First United Methodist Church in downtown Shreveport, the Alternate View Network is a telecommunications center that sends programming nationwide by way of its satellite uplink system. The church was founded in 1845 and has stood at the head of Texas Street since 1883. The present sanctuary building dates to 1913.

SHREVEPORT CAPTAINS

In 1995 the Shreveport Captains helped the city celebrate 100 years of local professional baseball. Playing at the city-owned Fair Grounds Field ball park, the locally owned club is a farm team of the San Francisco Giants and a member of the Texas League.

LOUISIANA STATE FAIR

The State Fair of Louisiana, founded in 1906, is the largest livestock exposition in the state. While following its traditional emphasis on exhibiting agriculture, livestock, and industry, the October event also entertains with concerts, rodeos, a carnival midway, and commercial exhibits and displays.

SPORTRAN TERMINAL

In the late 1940s, with America rebuilding after World War II, the city transportation system reached its peak, carrying 20 million passengers a year on its buses and electric trolleys. The SporTran Terminal, a tensioned-fabric canopy structure built in 1986, is the hub of the city bus system.

SCI-PORT DISCOVERY CENTER

The Sci-Port Discovery Center is a hands-on science museum for children. Currently located on Shreveport's downtown riverfront, the museum offers traveling and permanent exhibits, plus a KIDSPACE area for ages three to seven. A new permanent riverfront home for the center and an adjoining IMAX theater was in the planning stages in 1995.

CADDO PARISH COURTHOUSE

The Caddo Parish Courthouse is the third to stand on this site in downtown Shreveport. The first served as the Louisiana statehouse during the Civil War after first Baton Rouge and then a temporary capital at Opelousas fell to Union troops. The second, constructed in 1892, was replaced in 1928 by the current building, designed by Edward Neild. President Harry Truman was so impressed by the courthouse that he asked Neild to do reconstruction design work on the White House and to design the Truman Library in Independence, Missouri.

STRAND THEATRE

Opened in 1925 as a movie palace and vaudeville hall by Julian and A. D. Saenger and Simon Ehrlich, the magnificent Strand, at Crockett and Louisiana Streets, was the flagship of the renowned Saenger Brothers theater chain. After falling into disuse and disrepair in the 1970s, the Strand was acquired by a nonprofit corporation, restored to its former grandeur, and reopened in 1984. The corporation now runs it as a theater for the performing arts. The building was designed by Emile Weil, with the interior by Paul Heerwagen and Associates.

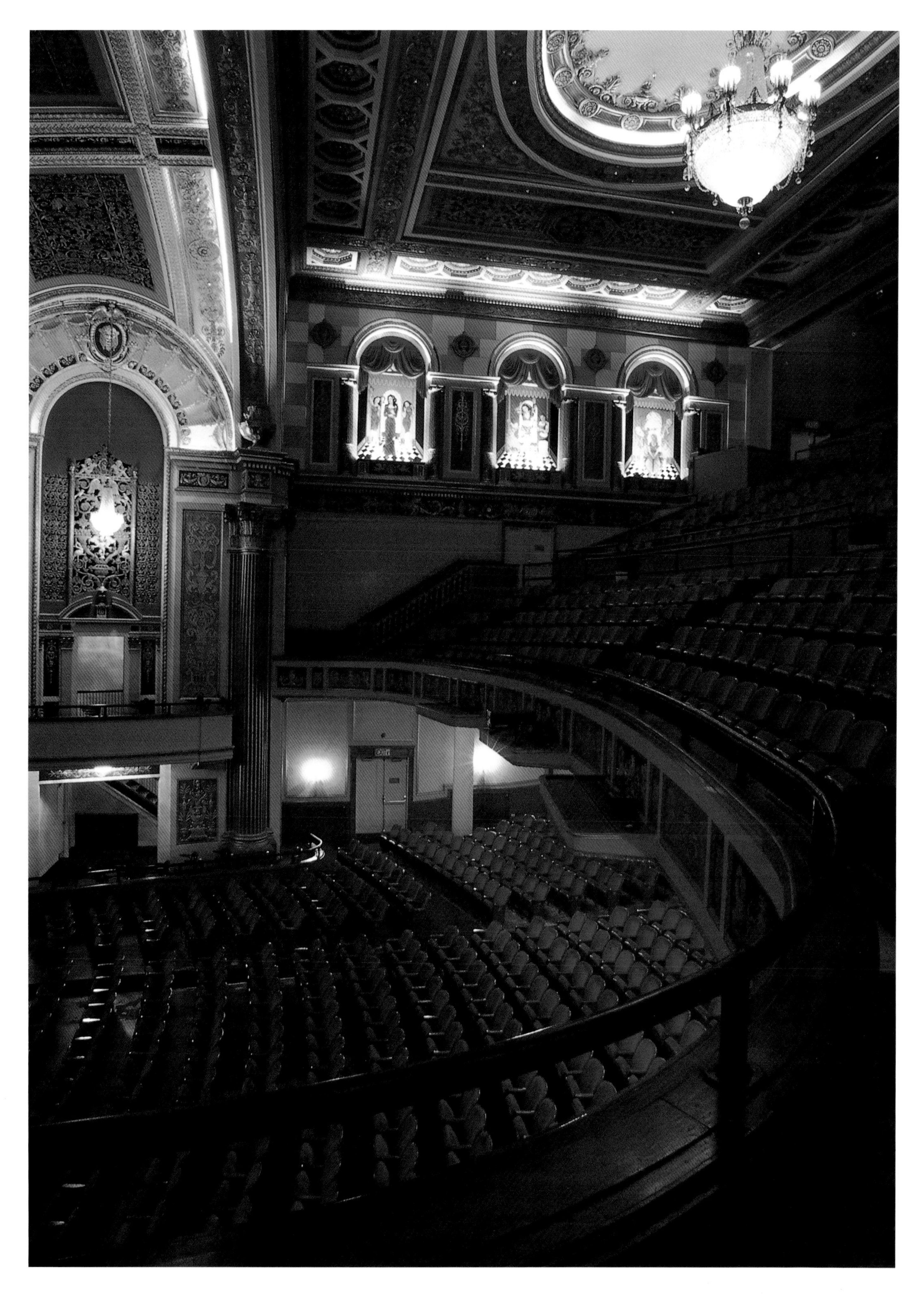

AT&T'S SHREVEPORT WORKS

In operation since 1965, AT&T's Shreveport Works, on Mansfield Road, builds business telecommunication systems and telephones for the world. At its employment peak in 1985, before extensive cutbacks began, the plant employed 7,800 workers.

FOREIGN TRADE ZONE

Legally outside the United States Customs Service's jurisdiction, this warehouse adjacent to AT&T is part of Shreveport's Foreign Trade Zone. Here local firms enjoy great tariff advantages in receiving goods such as telephone components from the Far East and, after assembly, exporting the finished products.

THE LEWIS HOUSE

The Lewis House, on Jordan Street, was built in 1898 and was long occupied by the family of early Shreveport druggist T. C. Lewis.

INTER CITY ROW MODERN DANCE COMPANY

The Inter City Row Modern Dance Company is a professional dance touring company based in Shreveport.

HAMEL'S AMUSEMENT PARK

Hamel's Amusement Park began in the 1960s as a small zoo operated by a local dairy family. In 1970 facilities for birthday parties were added. Today Hamel's has grown to become the largest amusement park in North Louisiana.

AT&T

FOURTH OF JULY CELEBRATION

Each year a large portion of the community gathers to celebrate the Fourth of July with an evening of picnics, live music, and fireworks.

(Below) EIGHTH AIR FORCE MUSEUM

The Eighth Air Force Museum, located at Barksdale Air Force Base, features the history of the base from 1933, of the 2d Bomb Wing from 1918, and of the Eighth Air Force from 1942.

This World War II B-17 bomber and Korean-era F-84 jet fighter are part of the museum's growing collection of historic aircraft.

BARKSDALE AIR FORCE BASE

Barksdale Air Force Base is the headquarters to both the Eighth Air Force and the 2d Bomb Wing, which flies the B-52H bombers. Also stationed at the Bossier City base is the 917th Fighter Wing Air Force Reserve. With 22,000 acres of Bossier Parish land purchased through sales of a 1929 Shreveport bond issue and donated to the United States Army, the War Department dedicated what was then known as Barksdale Field in 1933. Each spring Barksdale offers an open house to the public, with an air show and a large number of aircraft on static display.

DESERT STORM B-52

The first aircraft to leave the United States for Operation Desert Storm took off from Barksdale. Upon their return, the B-52s flew low to receive the community's welcome home.

(Below) Dawn maintenance at Barksdale

548D

(Overleaf) FOREST INDUSTRY

Shreveport and Bossier City are surrounded by an abundance of commercial forests, providing a large and renewable source of lumber and paper products. At the same time, local foresters, wildlife managers, and environmental consultants work together to preserve the ecological integrity, recreational quality, and aesthetic beauty of the forests.

THE TIMES

The Shreveport *Times* began publishing in 1871 and is today the only daily newspaper in Shreveport and Bossier City. A member of the Gannett newspaper group since 1977, the morning paper—now named simply *The Times*—is circulated throughout the region.

(Right) ILLINOIS CENTRAL GULF BRIDGE

The old Illinois Central Gulf Bridge (purchased in 1992 by Kansas City Southern) crosses the Red River near downtown Shreveport. It was built in 1916, replacing an 1884 bridge constructed by the Vicksburg, Shreveport and Pacific Railroad.

RECYCLING

Caddo Parish Middle Magnet School students recycle once a month with Shreveport's Recycling Program. Begun in 1992, the municipal program includes two full-service buy-back centers, a network of unattended drop-off sites, mobile recycling units, and a yard-waste composting service.

RED RIVER REVEL

The Red River Revel arts festival, initiated by the Shreveport Junior League in 1976 as a bicentennial gift to the city, offers eight days of visual and performing arts on the riverfront. The annual early-fall event also features a hands-on discovery center, a full program of children's art education, and a variety of lectures, workshops, and demonstrations by artists and performers. Dozens of food booths serve both local and international fare.

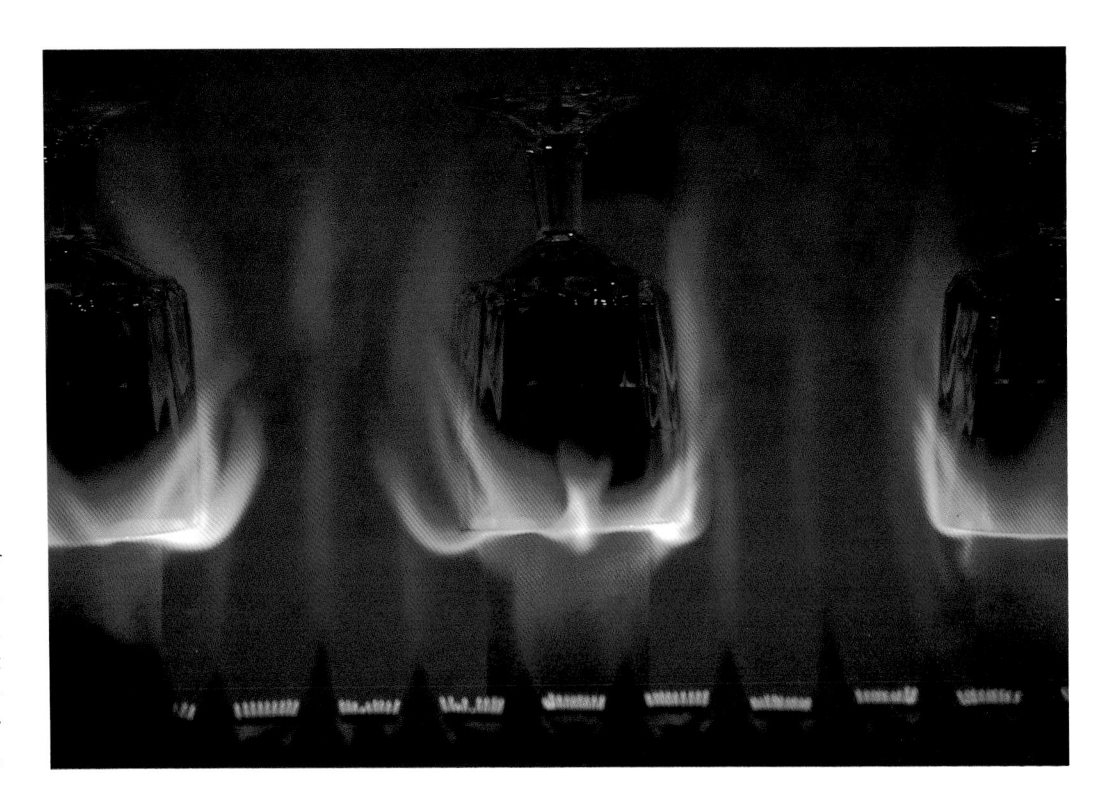

LIBBEY GLASS

In 1972 Libbey Glass, the oldest table-glassware maker in America, moved into the former Shreveport factory of Libby Owen Ford. At the time the factory began operation in 1922 to produce sheet glass, it was both the largest manufacturer and the largest employer in Shreveport.

(Right) HOLY TRINITY CATHOLIC CHURCH

Established in 1856, Holy Trinity was the first Catholic church in Caddo-Bossier. The current building, on Marshall Street in downtown Shreveport, was built in 1896 to replace a smaller structure. Holy Trinity has more than sixty stained-glass windows, five of which commemorate the heroism of five Catholic priests who died of yellow fever while caring for victims of the 1873 epidemic, which claimed some 760 lives in Shreveport.

Red River Revel

To THE MEMORY OF
FATHER
PIER RE
IN
IEUX
IN
1873
THE MEMORY OF REVEREND
J QUÉREMAIS
BORN IN RENNES
HE GAVE HIS LIFE DURING THE YELLOW FEVER EPIDEMIC SHREVEPORT 1873
ONE HAS
FRIENDS
THIS WINDOW
REST IN PEACE

(Left) ATLAS PROCESSING COMPANY

One of the oldest and largest inland refineries in the country, Atlas Processing Company processes approximately 50,000 barrels of crude oil daily. Founded in 1923 to service the area's booming oil industry, the refinery now operates as a subsidiary of Pennzoil Company.

Situated on 240 acres next to I-20, Atlas turns out a variety of products, among them gasoline, lubricating oil, refined petroleum wax, and specialty oils.

(Left) SHREVEPORT SYMPHONY ORCHESTRA

Founded in 1948, the Shreveport Symphony Orchestra presents a wide variety of classical, pops, and chamber music performances. The orchestra also provides an extensive in-school educational concert program throughout northwest Louisiana.

Ford Park

FOOD

Shreveport and Bossier City succeed on many fronts at living up to Louisiana's reputation for outstanding culinary fare. With restaurants serving everything from catfish to barbecue and from Tex-Mex to Italian, this community gives good eating high priority. Here, Chef Jimmy Johnston of the Horseshoe Casino offers a sample.

Chef
Johnston

SHREVEPORT PIRATES

In 1994 the Shreveport Pirates came into being as the southernmost team in the Canadian Football League. They play from June into November, with Independence Stadium as their home field.

CHAMPION LAKE PRO CLASSIC

A side effect of Captain Henry Miller Shreve's work on the Red River was the creation of a small cutoff lake in what is now southeast Shreveport. Home of the professional water-skiing tour's Champion Lake Pro Classic, the smooth waters have seen more world water-ski records fall than any other lake. The Pro Classic, with slalom skiing, distance jumping, and trick competitions, is held every July.

THOROUGHBREDS

Largely due to the presence of Louisiana Downs, northwest Louisiana quickly developed a thoroughbred horse-breeding industry. Here, a mare in the foaling barns of Franks Farms, just north of Shreveport, snuggles a foal only minutes old.

(Left) I-20, Bossier City, with Shreveport in the background

CROSS LAKE

The Cross Lake Bridge carries I-220 from Willow Point to loop around downtown Shreveport in the background *(above)*. Cross Lake provides both Shreveport's drinking-water supply and a place to unfurl a sail or two.

Hardtner Chapel, American Rose Center

AMERICAN ROSE CENTER

Home of the American Rose Society, the American Rose Center spreads over 118 acres—44 of them planted in roses—under the tall pines just west of Shreveport. The largest American garden dedicated to roses grows steadily larger through donations from rosarians across the country and boasts over 20,000 roses of more than 400 varieties, including the "Shreveport" rose.

The center is open from when the first roses bloom (late April or early May) to the end of October. From the weekend after Thanksgiving through New Year's Eve, the gardens reopen transformed into "Christmas in Roseland," a wonderland of lights and animated scenes amid the sleeping roses.

"Shreveport" roses, American Rose Center

(Right) SMITHERMAN HOUSE

This imposing Greek Revival mansion at Erie Street and Glen Iris was designed by Edward Neild for local oilman J. E. Smitherman and epitomizes the large homes built in and around Shreveport as a result of the oil boom of the 1920s and 1930s.

Adai Trail
Interpretive Bldg

ST. MARK'S EPISCOPAL CATHEDRAL

St. Mark's traces its origins to 1839, when Episcopal bishop Leonidas Polk visited Shreveport and conducted a service in the then-churchless frontier town. In 1959, after many years at what is now Holy Cross Episcopal Church downtown, the parish began worship in the present sanctuary in the Fairfield Historic District. St. Mark's became the seat of the bishop of the Diocese of Western Louisiana in 1990. Pictured is a performance by the Baroque Artists of Shreveport.

(Left) WALTER B. JACOBS MEMORIAL NATURE PARK

Just north of Cross Lake, this 160-acre pine-oak-hickory forest preserve encloses an interpretive building and five miles of nature trails. The "Adai Trail" is named for a branch of the Caddo Indians.

Walter B. Jacobs was president of the First National Bank of Shreveport from 1896 until his death in 1904.

MUNICIPAL AUDITORIUM/"LOUISIANA HAYRIDE"

Shreveport's Municipal Auditorium was the center for much of the local performing arts until the Civic Theater opened on the riverfront in 1965. Designed by Samuel Wiener and built in 1929, the art deco auditorium has long been admired for its elaborate ornamental brickwork.

The building is probably best known as the home of the "Louisiana Hayride." Called the "Cradle of the Stars," the show helped launch the careers of Hank Williams Sr., Johnny Horton, Slim Whitman, and Johnny Cash, among many others. But the most famous of all the voices to resonate within the auditorium was that of the young Elvis Presley, who from 1954 to 1956 performed eighty-four times on the Hayride. Here, an Elvis impersonator recreates the King's Hayride appearances.

The Hayride debuted in 1948 and peaked in popularity—largely through radio—during the mid-1950s. It ceased its weekly performances in 1960.

MT. CANAAN BAPTIST CHURCH

The congregation of Mt. Canaan Baptist Church, in the Allendale section of Shreveport, celebrates Easter Sunday.

HORSESHOE CASINO

Horseshoe Casino's 300-foot-long Queen of the Red is the largest local riverboat casino, with a capacity of 2,250 persons. Besides the vessel itself, the facility, located in Bossier City across the river from downtown Shreveport, includes an onshore pavilion housing several restaurants and a sports lounge.

Because of the Red River's unusual navigational characteristics, the three Shreveport-Bossier riverboat casinos are exempt from state law requiring such vessels to conduct cruises. Thus, aboard all three, the gaming is dockside twenty-four hours a day.

HORSESHOE
CASINO

49
EXIT 19A
NORTH
71
1
Spring St
Market St
EXIT ONLY

HIBERNIA
Spring St 1/2
Common St - La Ave 3/4
Fairfield Ave 1 1/4
BRIDGE MAY ICE IN COLD WEATHER

GENERAL MOTORS ASSEMBLY PLANT

The Shreveport Assembly Plant of General Motors Truck Group manufactures Chevrolet and GMC small pickups. The plant began operations in 1981 and has achieved a solid reputation for high quality, low cost, and efficiency. In late 1995, the plant added Isuzu small trucks to its line.

SHREVE MEMORIAL LIBRARY

The Shreve Memorial Library, shown here in its Christmas lights, occupies the old Federal Building, which dates to 1912 and once included the downtown Post Office. The library system has twenty branches.

SporTran terminal, Christmas

"Christmas in Roseland" at the American Rose Center, a highlight of the community's "December on the Red" holiday illumination.

OIL AND GAS EXPLORATION

The discovery of oil in the area at the turn of the century transformed Shreveport from a town into a city. Oil and gas exploration and production quickly became the cornerstone of the northwest Louisiana economy. Today the industry is not the dominant force it once was, but it still exerts a powerful influence.

LOGAN MANSION

This Victorian-era residence was designed by N. S. Allen and built in 1897 by L. R. Logan, prominent in the then-thriving local brewing industry. Located on Austin Place, a street known for its late-nineteenth-century homes, the mansion has housed a succession of radio stations since 1976.

OLD RIVER

A former channel of the Red River is now a quiet body of water named Old River in east Shreveport—and a beautiful place to watch the seasons change.

PUMPKIN SHINE ON LINE

Each October hundreds of jack-o'-lanterns illuminate the paths of Betty Virginia Park, on Line Avenue, during the Pumpkin Shine on Line neighborhood festival.

LINE AVENUE

Line Avenue looking south from Kings Highway. C. E. Byrd High School, Shreveport's oldest existing high school (1925), stands in the foreground.

Holiday in Dixie block party

Doo Dah Parade, Holiday in Dixie

HOLIDAY IN DIXIE

Holiday in Dixie, first celebrated in 1949, ushers in spring with a ten-day festival of parades, block parties, a cotillion ball, and dozens of other events. The festivities conclude with the annual Barksdale Air Force Base open house.

(Right) Barksdale Air Force Base open house

Classic Parade, Holiday in Dixie

HIBERNIA
BO DING SERVICE
AIL BONDS

OAK TREE, SLATTERY BOULEVARD

Undoubtedly the consensus favorite individual tree of Shreveporters, this live oak spreads its gnarled limbs across the front yard of a Slattery Boulevard home.

ISLE OF CAPRI CASINO

The Isle of Capri Casino features a tropical theme and a 30,000-square-foot riverboat gaming facility with a capacity of 1,650 people. A 37,000-square-foot pavilion houses three restaurants. The Bossier City casino operates in partnership with the Louisiana Downs racetrack.

HIGH-SCHOOL FOOTBALL

On autumn Friday nights, the stadium is the place to be. The lights go on, the partisan crowds pour in, and the pageantry and competition begin. Here, the Southwood Cowboys battle the Woodlawn Knights.

(Right) SOUTHERN UNIVERSITY AT SHREVEPORT

Located in northern Shreveport, this commuter school—part of the Southern University system—accepts students primarily from northwestern Louisiana through its open-admission policy. Its Science and Technology Division programs include the acclaimed Allied Health Program and Aviation Maintenance Program.

FIRST BAPTIST CHURCH

First Baptist Church, founded in 1845 and long a downtown landmark, moved into its South Highlands home in 1963. The church incorporated Dodd College *(on left)*, founded by and named for Dr. M. E. Dodd, pastor of the church from 1912 to 1950. From 1927 to 1942, Dodd College was a two-year liberal arts college for girls. Centenary College purchased the campus in 1943 and held classes there into the 1950s.

(Right) UNITED STATES COURT HOUSE

The U.S. District Court, U.S. Bankruptcy Court, and U.S. Court of Appeals for the Fifth Circuit moved into the new United States Court House in 1993.

UNITED STATES COURT HOUSE

SOUTH HIGHLAND MAGNET SCHOOL

At South Highland Elementary Academic and Performing Arts Magnet School, two children begin the day by raising the American flag.

(Right) SHREVEPORT LANDMARK

Begun in 1983 to rescue dilapidated homes in the Ledbetter Heights and Allendale neighborhoods, Shreveport Landmark used a combination of private and public funding to restore nearly two hundred houses, such as these on Alston Street. The agency now rents and manages these homes for low-income residents while also providing classes in literacy, home care, and daily-living skills.

(Left) KIRBY STREET

These homes on Kirby Street are within the Fairfield Historic District, one of six designated historic districts in Shreveport and Bossier City. The Fairfield District runs between Line and Southern Avenues and between Kings Highway and Olive Street.

BOSSIER CITY MUNICIPAL COMPLEX

The Bossier City Municipal Complex includes the Bossier City Police and Fire Departments, city government offices and courts, and the Bossier Civic Center.

LSU IN SHREVEPORT

Located in southeast Shreveport, Louisiana State University in Shreveport opened in 1967 on two hundred acres of former cotton fields as a two-year college. It became a four-year college in 1974. Now offering forty-five undergraduate majors and five graduate programs, the school serves the Ark-La-Tex primarily as a commuter campus for over 4,000 students. The university's four colleges are business administration, education, liberal arts, and sciences.

RE/M

RED RIVER RALLY

In late July the Red River Rally—"A Hot Air Balloon Uprising"—fills the skies with gigantic, colorful hot air balloons lazily floating over the cotton fields and neighborhoods of south Shreveport and Bossier City. Hosted by LSU in Shreveport, the weekend family festival is the largest summer event in the state.

HARRAH'S CASINO

Of Shreveport and Bossier City's three riverboat casinos, Harrah's Casino Shreveport is the only one on the Shreveport side of the Red River and has been a major catalyst in the revival of the city's waterfront. Harrah's first boat, the *Shreveport Rose*, which opened in 1994, was replaced at the end of that year by the larger *Shreve Star*, with a capacity of 1,400 passengers.

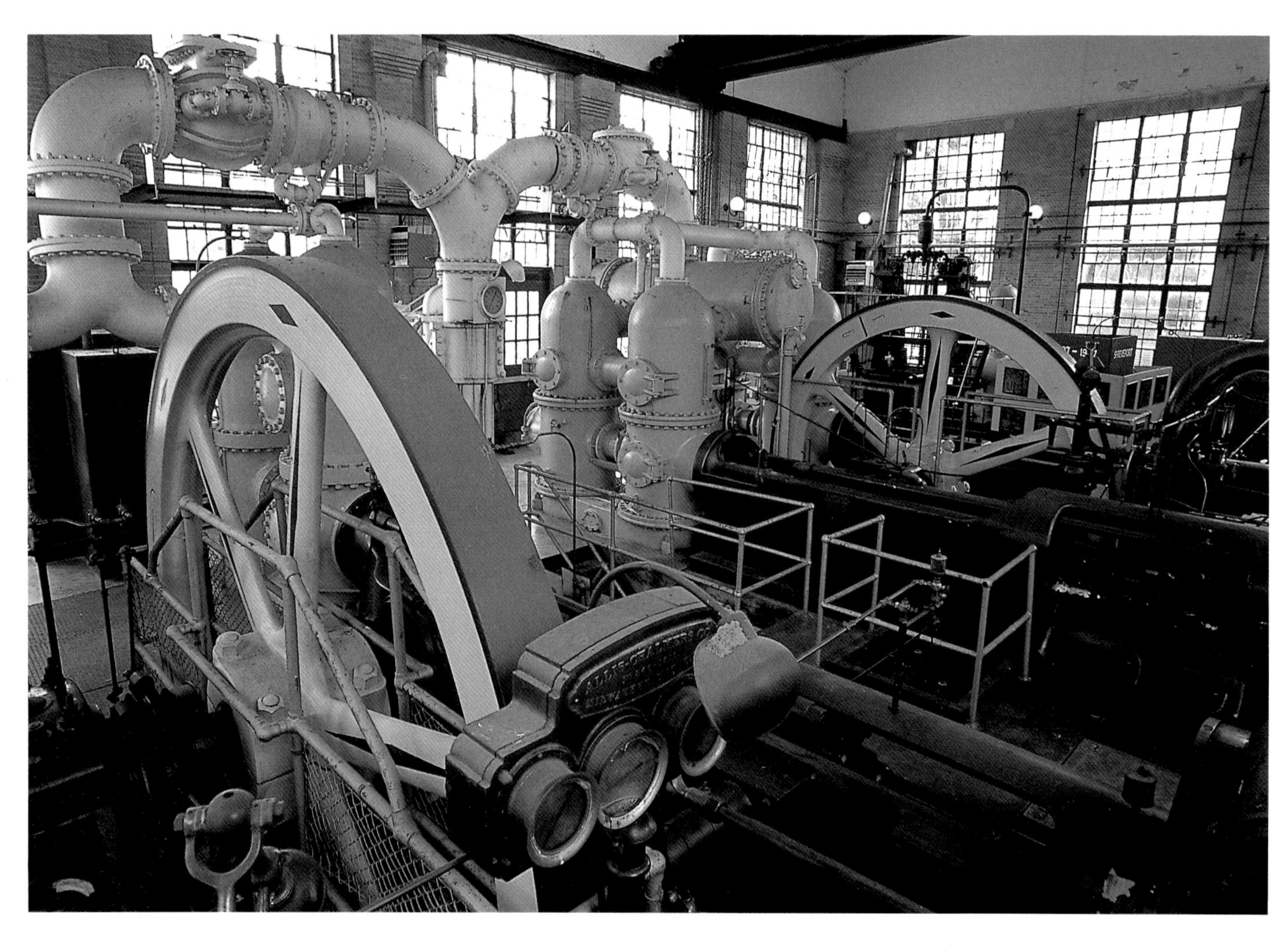

MCNEILL STREET PUMPING STATION

In post–Civil War Shreveport, drinking water and adequate water for fighting fires were in short supply. To solve both problems, the McNeill Street Pumping Station was built in 1887. It pulled water first from Cross Bayou, later from the Red River, and finally from Cross Lake.

The two large steam pumps, installed in 1920, continued in operation until they were retired in 1980, making this facility the last working steam pumping station in the country. It is the only National Historic Landmark listed in Caddo-Bossier.

B'NAI ZION TEMPLE

As part of his bar mitzvah, signifying attainment of the age of duty and responsibility in the Jewish religion, a young man reads from the 750-year-old Torah at the B'nai Zion Temple, on Southfield Road. Founded in 1859, the temple occupied a downtown location at 802 Cotton Street from 1915 until moving to the present site in 1956.

BOSSIER PARISH COMMUNITY COLLEGE

Bossier Parish Community College, founded in 1967, is a two-year junior college offering degrees and certificate programs in traditional academics as well as continuing education and specialized vocational-training classes. The commuter school also houses the Criminal Justice Institute for police training.

LOUISIANA STATE EXHIBIT MUSEUM

The Louisiana State Exhibit Museum, adjacent to the State Fair-grounds, showcases the social and cultural history of northwest Louisiana. In addition to housing the state's largest collection of Native American artifacts, the museum contains a series of twenty-two dioramas depicting Louisiana's industry and agriculture. The circular building, designed by Edward Neild, opened in 1939.

(Overleaf) Bossier City Municipal Complex with Christmas lights

CIVIC
CENTER

Master Mechanics
226-4600
CAR WASH
ABC
XEROX
ONLY

OAKLAND CEMETERY

Shreveport's oldest official cemetery, Oakland was chartered by the city in 1849—although the earliest marked grave is dated 1842. At least sixteen Shreveport mayors and many other early Shreveport citizens are buried here. The cemetery lies adjacent to the Municipal Auditorium.

(Left) YOUREE DRIVE/VA HOSPITAL

In a northward view along Youree Drive from Kings Highway, the Overton Brooks Veterans Administration Medical Center, opened in 1949, is at the upper right.

MUDBUG MADNESS

Each spring South Louisiana's Cajun heritage is celebrated in the four-day Mudbug Madness festival. Both traditional Cajun music and foot-stomping zydeco combine with a dozen varieties of spicy crawfish dishes to create a party atmosphere on the riverfront.

FIRST PRESBYTERIAN CHURCH

First Presbyterian Church, founded in 1845, began worship at its Jordan Street building in 1926, after moving from its downtown location where the Beck Building now stands. First Presbyterian, Antioch Baptist Church, and Noel Methodist Church are the only local churches with their original curved wooden pews, now virtually irreplaceable.

NIKE SHREVEPORT OPEN

Spring brings the Nike Shreveport Open, a PGA development-tour tournament, to Southern Trace Country Club, one of the premier courses in the South. Proceeds from the event benefit local charities.

(Overleaf) TEXAS STREET BRIDGE

Officially named for Huey Long and then-governor O. K. Allen and completed in 1933, the Long-Allen Bridge is commonly known as the "Texas Street Bridge."

In 1993 artist Rockne Krebbs transformed the bridge into a work of art with neon lights attached to the framework, searchlights at both ends, and a colorful fiber-optic-and-neon "gateway" on the Shreveport side. The lighting debuted that New Year's Eve. In 1995 matching neon lighting was added to the bridge's underside, illuminating a pedestrian connector between Texas Street and the Riverfront.

E-911

The Caddo Parish E-911 Center handles emergency communications to the Shreveport Police and Fire Departments and the Caddo Sheriff's Department. All 911 calls for emergency assistance are received at the Texas Avenue location, where dispatchers order up the appropriate aid. The building also serves as the emergency-operations center for Caddo-Bossier Civil Defense.

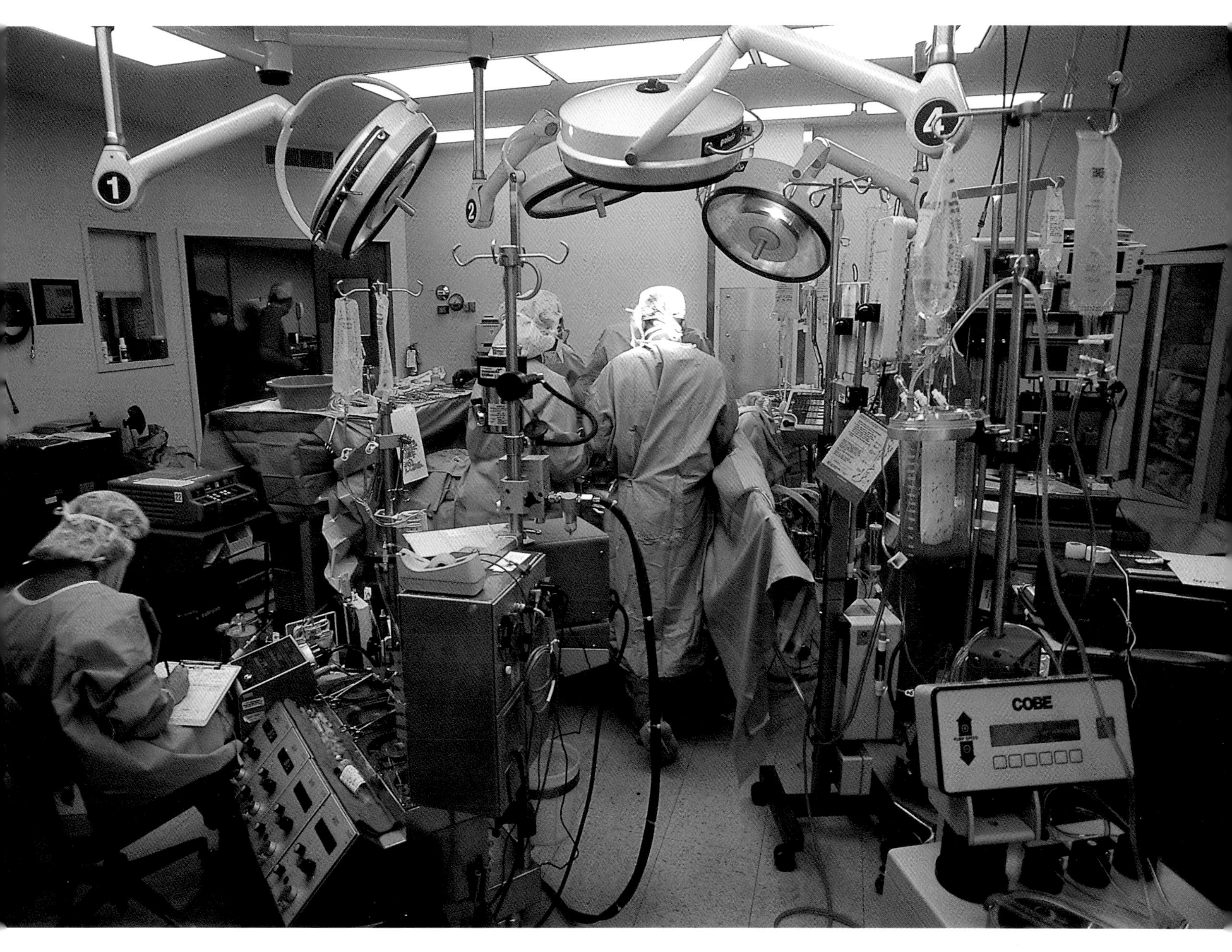

WILLIS-KNIGHTON MEDICAL CENTER

Begun in 1925 as the Tri-State Sanitarium, Willis-Knighton Medical Center, on Greenwood Road, has become one of the largest health-care providers in the area. The Willis-Knighton Health System now includes the Center for Women's Health, Willis-Knighton South, the Steen-Hall Eye Institute, and the Health and Fitness Center.

In 1990, Willis-Knighton began a joint venture with the LSU Medical Center to form the Regional Transplant Center for heart, heart-lung, liver, pancreas, and kidney transplants. The surgical team shown here is performing a heart transplant.

BOOTHILL SPEEDWAY

Boothill Speedway roars to life on weekends from March through October. Located just west of Shreveport, the half-mile dirt track offers five classes of racing but is primarily known for "I.M.C.A. modified" and "late model" competitions.

MANSFIELD ROAD

Mansfield Road was once merely the road between Shreveport and Mansfield but has become the major commercial thoroughfare for southwest Shreveport.

SHREVEPORT OPERA

Founded in 1949, Shreveport Opera produces at least four main stage events each year and an education program for area schools. Pictured is a production of Verdi's *Aïda* in the Civic Theater.

SAMUEL WIENER HOUSE

In 1937 Samuel G. Wiener designed this Longleaf Drive residence. Wiener and his brother William were American pioneers of the International style of architecture.

INDEPENDENCE BOWL

Each December, two college teams battle it out in a postseason football game in Independence Stadium. First played in 1976 to coincide with the nation's bicentennial, the Independence Bowl today caps a week-long lineup of special events in Shreveport and Bossier City.

In the background is Fair Park High School, Shreveport's second-oldest, and at right is Hirsch Memorial Coliseum.

SCOTTISH RITE CATHEDRAL

The Scottish Rite Cathedral, commonly referred to as the Scottish Rite Temple, is used for meetings and social functions of the Scottish Rite Masons in the Shreveport-Bossier area. Designed by Edward Neild and completed in 1917, the Cotton Street building also houses a speech, hearing, and language-disorder clinic for small children. The room pictured here is the library.

KCS RAIL YARD

The Doremus Yard in north Shreveport is the hub of operations for the Kansas City Southern Railway Company. The yard also contains KCS's main repair shop for its diesel locomotive engines.

SLATTERY HOUSE

The Slattery House, built in 1903 on Fairfield Avenue, is one of the last remaining examples of the residential design work of N. S. Allen, one of the leading southern architects of the time.

HIBERNIA
LDS

INDEX